GET BACK UP

Simple Steps To Success And Happiness
When Life Knocks You Down

MARK LLEWHELLIN

Book 4 in the
Mark Llewhellin
Success and Happiness Series

DEDICATION

This book is dedicated to the love of my life, my little miracle, Léon James Llewhellin, who I love more than anyone in the world. You are kind, thoughtful, well balanced and you are already achieving great things in your life!

Words cannot describe how much I love you and how proud I am of the person you are.

I also dedicate this book to you, the reader. Life will knock you down. GET BACK UP!

GET TWO OF MARK'S BOOKS FOR FREE

Join Mark's team for information on new books along with special offers and pick up a FREE copy of Mark's 5 star reviewed books:

'The Underdog' and 'Delusions Of Grandeur.'

Details can be found at the end of this book.

TABLE OF CONTENTS

INTRODUCTION

*"You gain strength, courage and confidence by every experience
in which you really stop to look fear in the face. You can say to
yourself, I lived through this horror. I can take the next thing
that comes along."*
– Eleanor Roosevelt

Get Back Up

Have you ever gone through challenging times in your life?

Sometimes in life everything can go right for you.

You can ride on the crest of a wave, you're using the law of attraction, you're grateful for everything you've got, you're positive that things will continue to get better and before you know it... all hell breaks loose!

You lose your job, your house, your relationship breaks up, you lose a loved one, and through no fault of your own, everything goes wrong!

It's like one minute, you were on your beautiful ship of life and living the dream, and the next minute, from out of nowhere, a violent storm hits your ship and you get emotionally tossed from side-to-side and you're holding on for dear life!

When you get a quick second to think, you think about how things have got so bad, and you say,

"God, why are you doing this to me?"

You have two options.

1. You let life's ship throw you from side-to-side, and give up.

or

2. You focus, grab the ship's wheel, hold on, and steer towards a better life!

Your navigation systems are broke, you're confused, you're cheesed off, and you're no longer sure if you're going in the right direction!

You were following the rules to success and you can't understand why this has happened to you.

Well, that's life for you!

The good news is; when your life goes off the rails, you can take control of things and ultimately... Get back up!

CHAPTER 1

SURVIVING DARK TIMES

"Just as the acorn contains the mighty oak tree, the self has everything it needs to fulfil its destiny. When the inner conditions are right, it naturally emerges."
– Derek Rydall

So here I am, lying on the sofa watching the computer animated science-fiction comedy 'Cloudy With a Chance of Meatballs' with my son Léon.

There's a part in the movie where the main character has been a success and shortly afterwards things go wrong and he's hiding in a barrel in a state of depression.

If you've lived long enough and you've been through enough, you'll get to a point where things aren't so great and you're struggling with life.

If you've ever experienced this, then great, welcome to the club!

No matter who you are, or what you've achieved, there will be times in your life where you feel less than great, and you're not happy with the way things have turned out or the way things are going right now.

It's an unpleasant and lonely place to be, and it's not somewhere where you want to stay.

I wish there could be a quick fix for feeling like this, but the truth is you will have to work on things, you will have to change your habits and also change the way you look at things.

Are you in an unpleasant situation?

Is the situation you're in difficult to get out of?

Even if you can't see it the chances are,

"There's a bright future waiting for you!"

Your challenging experiences are things that can help other people, so it may be time to reach out, bring your experience and knowledge to the table, and use it for the greater good!

Sometimes, we can feel overwhelmed with everything going on around us; there are so many things to do in so little time.

When you look at a jungle, it comprises thousands of trees, which are called a canopy.

So, how do these thousands of trees grow?

Everything starts in the darkness!

Life begins in the darkness, and it's a struggle to survive whether you're a tiny seed surrounded by massive trees in darkness, or whether it's a human sperm fighting its way past millions of other sperm trying to create life and become something.

Dipterocarp trees in the jungle can spend many years on the ground, not growing very much, just waiting there for an opportunity.

When the time is right, a gap will open up to the trees below from the trees above.

This could be in the form of branches falling off, or leaves falling off from the trees above which gives the seeds, the plants, and the trees below the ability to grow.

Even though it spends much of its time in darkness, with enough light and the right conditions around it, the Dipterocarp tree can grow to colossal heights of above 150 feet!

The seed will need water, sunlight, and the right temperature to grow, and it's the same with us as human beings!

There will still be darkness in your life, but it's important to cling onto that light!

That light in our lives could be a friend supporting us and lifting our spirits.

It could be listening to music you love.

It could be reading a book like this one.

Maybe it's an inspirational movie, or something else that helps you through a challenging time.

Look for the light, hold on to it, and get back up!

CHAPTER 2

GET OFF THE CANVAS WHEN YOU'VE BEEN KNOCKED DOWN

"He who is not courageous enough to take risks will accomplish nothing in life."
– Muhammad Ali

There were several significant events in 1976, such as:

- The first commercial supersonic flights by Concorde began.

- Steve Jobs and Steve Wozniak got together and created Apple.

- The British Rail InterCity 125 High-Speed Train entered service.

- Fidel Castro became the President of Cuba.

- NASA unveiled its first space shuttle.

And…

- The much loved British comedian legend and star of the 'Carry On' movies Sid James died on stage at the Sunderland Empire having suffered a fatal heart attack.

However, as one much loved actor passes, an unknown actor in the United States was about to get his first shot at the title in the movie industry.

On the 6th July 1946, a baby boy was born in the Hell's Kitchen neighbourhood of Manhattan, New York City.

During the birth, his mother had complications, and he had to be taken out with two pairs of forceps, which accidentally severed a nerve and caused paralysis in a part of his face.

He would live with this facial defect for the rest of his life!

From an early age, the young man wanted to be in the movies, he wasn't very good at school, so he dropped out and worked in a dockyard.

Many people thought he didn't have a lot going for him and didn't think he would achieve much in life.

His dream was to become an actor, but people thought he didn't look right, and he didn't speak properly. So whenever he would go for a casting audition for an acting role he would be rejected time and time again.

Eventually, through blatant persistency, he got a role in his first movie. He was only in it for about 20 seconds, but it was still a result!

He was struggling to pay his rent and couldn't afford to put the heating on; his wife would shout at him and tell him to get a normal job, but he wanted to become a successful actor, so that's what he put all of his time into.

He believed that if he got a regular job, he would lose his hunger for acting and was afraid of getting stuck in a rut, so he burned all of his bridges!

One day he was freezing cold, so he went to the public library because there was heating in the building.

In the library he saw a book in front of him that caught his eye; the book was by the author Edgar Allan Poe, and he loved it.

This literary encounter led to him wanting to write and act.

He wrote a load of screenplays, but nothing worked. He was so broke, he didn't have $50 to his name, but after a lot of persistence he sold a script called 'Paradise Alley' for $100.

He was delighted with this because $100 back then was a lot of money to him, and he finally believed he was on his way to bigger and better things.

However, the money soon went, and he ended up selling his wife's jewellery so they could get by.

These were tough times, but the one thing that he loved more than anything in the world was his dog, because his dog gave him unconditional love.

However, he was going further into a desperate financial crisis, so he made the heart-breaking decision to take his dog to a nearby liquor store and tried to sell it to people walking by.

He tried to sell his dog for $50 but only ended up getting $25.

When he walked away from that situation he cried his eyes out and felt it was the worst day of his life!

He had virtually no money, and he just separated from the one thing that he loved more than anything, his dog.

He kept going for roles and after lots of rejection finally got cast in a movie called 'The Lords of Flatbush,' which got critical acclaim.

But even after that movie, he still didn't get the break he

so desperately wanted.

Two weeks later, he went to watch a fight featuring the World Heavyweight Boxing Champion Muhammad Ali, who was fighting a 30 – 1 underdog called Chuck Wepner.

What nobody expected was for Wepner to knock the champion down and last the distance!

The young man was so inspired by Wepner's performance, he went back to his apartment and wrote a story about a fighter who was a massive underdog.

He used the fight as a metaphor for life, where one man fought the odds, took his shot, did something everyone thought was impossible and went the distance!

The young man lived in an apartment that was only 8ft x 9ft, but even though his room was tiny, he found a positive in it, which was that there was little distraction in that room.

He would spend hours on end writing on his note pad, and the one thing he was most interested in was an unrealised dream.

He thought about the people that didn't get the recognition and the success that they could have had in life and thought about how he could make a story out of that.

His mind went into overdrive, and within the space of only three days he came up with the script of an underdog getting a shot in life and doing well.

The young man knew that it wasn't the finished article, but it was around 90 pages long and that was a good start.

In the initial script, his protagonist was a very dark character, and the main character's coach and mentor, who was called 'Mickey', was a foul-mouthed racist in that first draft.

When he showed it to his wife, she told him that she didn't like the script because it was too dark; the young man agreed with her and rewrote it several times.

He had completed the script, but he had told no movers and shakers in the film industry about it and wanted to get a part in another movie, so he went on a casting call, but at the end of his audition they decided not to give him the part.

As the young man was walking towards the door feeling rejected, he turned around and told the casting agent, "I don't know if it matters, but I do a bit of writing and I'm writing something about boxing."

The casting agent looked at him and said: "Bring it around."

When the young man said that to the casting agent, little did he know, that that encounter was about to change his entire life; that young man's name is Sylvester Stallone!

This is an important part of succeeding!

If nobody knows about you or nobody knows what you are working on, then you'll get nobody to come onboard and help you with your project or your dream.

To the credit of the casting agents, they didn't dismiss what the young Stallone had said.

Okay, it's very easy to take somebody like Sylvester Stallone seriously now, but back then nobody knew who he was.

However, the casting agents were always looking out for new opportunities, and if they had never said the words "bring it around," then their life, Stallone's life and the lives of many people around the world, (who have been inspired by the Rocky movies) would have all been worse off for it!

The agents were very enthusiastic about the script, but the last thing they wanted was for Stallone to play the part of Rocky, because nobody knew who he was back then.

They believed in the script, but they wanted a big movie star to play the part of Rocky, such as Burt Reynolds or Robert Redford, not an unknown struggling actor.

Today it's almost impossible to visualise somebody like Burt Reynolds or Robert Redford or anybody else playing the part of Rocky, apart from Sylvester Stallone.

They offered Stallone $25,000 for his script, and when he refused, they offered him $100,000 for the script.

However, the condition was that it would not allow him to play the part of Rocky. All they wanted was the script, and that was it!

How many people do you know that would have walked away happy with $100,000 or even $25,000?

Most people back then would have been happy to write something over the space of a few weeks and get paid $25,000 for their work, but Stallone believed this was a once in a lifetime opportunity and he wanted to play the part of Rocky more than anything else.

At that time in his life, Stallone had only $106 in the bank!

He was also driving around in an old banger of a car that cost him $40, but it broke down, so he had to take the bus to work.

Selling his dog broke his heart, and he was at an all-time low with his finances.

When he was offered $100,000 he could have easily taken the money as most people would, but he refused.

The offers kept coming!

Stallone got an offer for $150,000, then $175,000, then $250,000!

At this point, Stallone's head was spinning!

It then went up to $330,000 and then $360,000!

But he thought to himself, he had managed poverty pretty well, and he realised he didn't need much money to live on.

He realised that if he sold the script, and the movie became a blockbuster, he would regret his decision for the rest of his life!

Stallone stuck his heels in and insisted that he would be the main actor!

Eventually, they gave in and offered Stallone the part, but on the condition that he would only get $35,000.

What do you think he did with that money when he got it?

The first thing Stallone did was go back to the liquor store where he sold his dog to a passer-by, and buy his dog back.

He showed up for three straight days, waiting for the man to pass with his dog.

When he eventually saw the man walking with his dog (roughly a month and a half after he sold him his dog), Stallone approached him and said: "Can you remember me? I'm the guy that sold you the dog."

The man replied: "Yes, of course I remember you!"

Stallone explained the situation and told the man that he was so broke he needed to find some money so he could eat.

Even though the man had bought the dog for $25, Stallone

offered him $100 to buy his dog back, but the man said: "No way, he's my dog now, you can't buy him back!"

However, the young Stallone was determined to get his dog (called Butkus) back, and offered the man $500 to which the response was: "No way!"

Stallone then offered $1,000, and the man said: "There is no amount of money on this earth that will get your dog back for you!"

However, Stallone knew what he wanted, and he would not give up.

In the end Stallone paid the man $15,000 out of his $35,000 and also gave the man a brief part in the Rocky movie!

When they started filming, Stallone had to do a lot of running; through shopping malls, ghettos, factories and the iconic 72 stone steps.

He was finding the amount of running increasingly difficult, but the cameraman said that it was important to see his suffering, as it would come across in the movie.

Stallone suffered with shinsplints, broke a finger, and also damaged his hands when hitting meat hanging up in the cooler.

The director and producer wanted $2.5 million to make a movie, and if you know anything about making movies, you'll know that $2.5 million is peanuts! Even back in the 1970s.

However, the production company didn't want to put much money into it and settled on providing just under $1 million to make the movie, as they didn't want to gamble on this unknown actor called Sylvester Stallone.

With such a limited budget, Stallone asked many friends and family if they could come in as extras to help out!

In just about every movie you see these days, the clothes have been bought and are picked for the actors, but with Rocky they couldn't afford a wardrobe for everybody, so the cast had to provide their own.

When they first started looking for other actors to play alongside Sylvester Stallone, they needed somebody to play the world champion boxer Apollo Creed.

They auditioned real boxers such as Ken Norton and Joe Frazier but going in the ring with a former world champion was too testing for Stallone and that didn't work out.

They kept looking and auditioned many, but they couldn't

find anybody suitable.

Finally, they found a former American football player by the name of Carl Weathers.

Carl was introduced to the producers and the writer (Stallone himself) and started to read the script with the director watching them both.

Weathers had no idea that Stallone was not only the writer but was also the main character and said: "I would do much better if I had a real actor talking back to me, so who's playing Rocky?"

When they told him that the writer is also the main actor, I guess it was a bit of an enlightening experience for Weathers.

Although many people would have found what Weathers said to Stallone insulting if they were in Stallone's shoes, Stallone didn't.

He loved the cockiness and arrogance of Weathers and convinced everybody else on the team that Weathers should get the part of Apollo Creed.

Another character in the movie is the part of Rocky's brother-in-law Paulie (played by Burt Young).

Paulie is the person in the movie that hates his life, he hates everybody else and he hates that he hasn't been given a big break in life.

He feels sorry for himself constantly.

We all know someone in our lives that thinks like this.

The problem is, if you play the victim in real life, you will always be the victim!

You will never be the winner.

You will be a victim of one circumstance or another throughout your life, but it's what you do with that that will that make you a winner or a loser!

There was no time to waste, and they needed to finish filming the entire movie within the space of just one month to stay on budget, which was a limited time frame as far as movie making goes!

The production company needed to be as efficient as it could be, and on some days there were over 60 set ups in one day with very few second takes, as they didn't have the time or the budget!

That pressure brought out the resourcefulness and the

creative genius of both the actors and the crew!

If you have ever seen any of the Rocky movies, you will know how impactful and important the music is to the story.

However, there was a budget of only $25,000 for the entire music score, i.e. the composition, the musicians, the studios, the tape, and anybody else that was involved that needed to be paid.

A young composer called Bill Conti asked the director John G. Avildsen if he could see the movie before he composed the music, but Avildsen told him that he couldn't, as there wasn't the money to provide a projector and a projectionist at that point.

Conti knew he had to create a piece of music that showed an underdog fighter getting a shot at the title, and possibly even winning the title.

However, the inspirational anthem that Bill Conti and his team put together within a short time frame, with minimal funds, was sheer genius and is immediately recognisable all around the world as the Rocky theme!

Cameraman Garrett Brown knew that he couldn't run around with a handheld camera that would capture the

Rocky training properly. The equipment was cumbersome and the result would be a shaky recording.

Brown, who was also an amateur inventor, was already working on a concept that would be called Steadicam. This invention enabled a cameraman to wear a camera using body straps and a gimbal, in order to control the balance of the device.

He brought his prototype to the shoots for Rocky and it worked a treat!

The smooth action shots of Stallone in full physical flow were a first for cinematography.

That is the way a lot of inventions are born; they are born out of necessity!

Without the Steadicam, one of the most iconic scenes of Stallone's entire movie career would have been missed!

If you haven't already guessed what the scene is, it's the one with Rocky in his horrendous looking grey tracksuit running up the 72 stone steps leading up to the Philadelphia Museum of Art.

The cameraman pans the camera around Stallone and unscripted, Stallone dances on the spot and throws his arms into the air, as if to celebrate a victory.

As you can imagine with a tight time frame and no spare cash, there was sometimes tension behind-the-scenes.

At one point Stallone said to everybody that he would love it if Apollo Creed came out of the corner (in the ring) and then throw four big right-handers at Rocky.

It upset the stunt coordinator, and he said in reality it would never happen!

However, Stallone knew it would add suspense and make an impressive scene.

The stunt coordinator was right, and in reality a boxer would never come out of the corner and throw four right-hand shots, one after the other!

The stunt coordinator quit there and then!

Even though the stunt coordinator had a point about the validity of the scene to professional boxing, it became a powerful and symbolic turning point in the movie that I can still remember to this day. At the time of writing, I haven't watched Rocky for over 15 years!

What is not apparent to most people when they watch the

movie is that Stallone and Weathers had hardly any boxing experience prior to starting the film!

Nevertheless, they were both boxing fans and knuckled down (pardon the pun), learning their moves every day and practising relentlessly.

It was filmed from start to finish in just 28 days!

The cast and crew all wanted to release the movie into the cinemas that year, but the distribution company, United Artists, had other priorities.

They wanted other films that they believed would be a bigger box office success to be released before Rocky.

When the film was released, a New York Times movie critic also gave Rocky a scathing review. So, it wasn't the best of starts!

Some of the early reviews mirrored the movie when Creed keeps knocking Rocky down, again and again!

Most fighters would have stayed down after such a battering, but with Rocky, he kept on coming back for more!

In the movie, after Rocky got back up, Creed just shook

his head as if to say, "Why the heck doesn't this guy just stay down, he suffered more than anybody else I fought with. He shouldn't be able to go on!"

That's the same with life!

At some point, someone will knock you down physically or mentally, but you've just got to keep getting back up!

As long as you get back up, stay focused, and stay positive about the result that you want to achieve, you will eventually break through!

From Stallone's original script for Rocky, only 10% of it made it into the final movie!

He learnt a lot on set and realised that tweaks were needed to make the film flow better.

In the movie, Rocky doesn't win the fight, but he shows the world his heart and his determination, so in return he gains respect, not only from others, but also from himself! Self-worth is key to fulfilment in life.

If you don't try to better yourself, you'll never know the euphoria you can feel from overcoming personal obstacles!

After they released the film, Stallone said that he didn't expect for it to become a big hit.

As he had no benchmark to compare it to, he believed that it was just going to be a nice little movie.

When the cast and the makers of Rocky showed up at the Director's Guild, there were roughly 900 people there to watch it.

While Stallone was watching the movie with the esteemed audience, he felt the movie wasn't being received well.

When the movie ended, the audience got up and walked out! There was no clapping or any sign that they enjoyed it.

Stallone sat there on his own feeling deflated, humiliated, and sad. He felt like a complete failure!

He then, feeling like total shit, got out of his seat, left the auditorium, and started walking down a flight of stairs towards the exit.

However, by the time he got to the top of the stairs he couldn't believe his eyes when he saw 900 people waiting for him in the lobby!

He was met with a thunderous applause.

And the rest as they say, is history!

At the Academy Awards in 1976, they nominated Rocky for 10 Oscars!

It won Best Picture, Best Film Editor, and the Best Director Award. Rocky also won at the Golden Globe Awards and made history as the first sports movie to win Best Picture!

And it also grossed $225 million in global box office receipts, which was over 200 times more than it cost to make… an incredible achievement!

Stallone later said,

"The Rocky philosophy is that people want to be the champion of their own life; it's this symbol about not giving up, and your dreams can come true!"

Get Back Up

CHAPTER 3

FAILING

"I learned so much of my wilderness, outdoor, survival stuff through failure, through getting things wrong."
– Bear Grylls

In the summer of 2015, my friend Toby Ellis started a fitness class called Body Funk Fitness.

The idea behind it was a DJ would play music in a nightclub and me and another instructor would take the class.

It was a kind of mix between Insanity and a U.S. Marine static workout with star jumps (jumping jacks), press-ups, abdominal work, running on the spot, etc.

A few weeks after we started, the other instructor left to go on a course, so it was just me and Toby left to make it work. We had a few people turn up at the beginning, but many never came back, and it failed.

There's no doubt that some people who wanted us to fail were glad it never worked out for us, but I never saw it as much of a failure.

Ok, so we never really made any money on it, but I got a workout out of it myself, and it provided me with another opportunity to talk in front of a group of people, so there were positives to come out of it!

There is almost always something good to come out of a situation when you've failed, and if you have failed at something, then at least you gave it a shot!

It's hardly the end of the world, and there are lots more opportunities out there for you to take advantage of.

Sometimes things won't work out for you, but it can be a blessing for things to come.

The week after Body Funk Fitness failed, I did my first interview with an entrepreneur called Ozana Giusca in London.

Instead of myself being interviewed about my running achievements, the tables had turned, and I was now living my dream of interviewing successful people.

The next day, I posted the first part of the interview onto Facebook, where it received over 400 views. The dream that I had when I first listened to Martyn Lewis interviewing Anthony Hopkins had become a reality.

I felt this was another string to my bow.

When I first started interviewing people, it was all new to me, so I had no real idea of what to do to create a successful interview.

I didn't understand about the lighting, how to sit, who the camera should focus on, how I would get great sound quality etc... but I believed there would be some great content for the viewers.

Even though I gained no financial reward from it, I absolutely loved it!

After the first three interviews, I felt as if this was one of my callings in life. There were mistakes made, but I learned fast, and you can do the same with something you've always dreamed of doing.

The other thing I did was to keep moving forward with plans for other projects; opportunities are everywhere when you look for it! Seek and you shall find.

Although failure is an initial kick in the privates, you can recover pretty quickly and move on, so don't wallow in self-pity, get off your arse, pick yourself up and move on!

You also have to remember that there are people out there

who need you to be strong for them, show people that you can bounce back from failure and they will respect you for it.

There are many high achievers who say that they have less respect for people who have never failed because it's the failures that can show your true character.

So never be afraid to take on big challenges and when you do fail, always, always, get back up!

CHAPTER 4

MASTER YOUR MIND

*"The mind is its own place and can make a heaven of hell,
a hell of heaven."*
– John Milton

I've thought long and hard over the years about what the greatest achievement is, and I concluded that mastering your thoughts is the greatest achievement of them all!

Sure you could become a billionaire, you could break a world record, you could travel the world and experience all of the things on your bucket list, but if you're not enjoying doing these things and you're not happy in life, then what's the point?

The billionaire that's unhappy can be just as unhappy as the unhappy guy living in poverty. On the flip side of that, the guy living in a third world country with very little money and is happy, is a much 'richer' guy than the unhappy billionaire!

I'm talking about inner riches that come from a certain state of mind, no matter what your situation is.

Many people think that this mindset is only attainable to

Zen types and Buddhist masters, but the reality is, you can take control of your state of mind, and that starts with being aware that you can alter your state if you really want to!

Regrets are one thing that hold people back in life, but you can never change the past. Logically, we know we shouldn't have regrets, but we have all regretted something we've done, even if we only regretted it for a moment.

Mastering your mind is a skill, and you can learn how to overcome things, live for today and look forward to the future.

Ask yourself the questions: "Do I want to relive my past all the time?" and "Do I want to relive that feeling of regret every single day?"

You may have seen the movie Groundhog Day where Bill Murray wakes up on the same day every morning.

Every day, he tries to correct mistakes that he's made, and at the end of the movie, he achieves what he wants by winning the heart of the woman he loves.

For us, each day is different, but if we let it, we can wake up each day with our mind in prison thinking about the past and what we should have done to correct it.

The past is the past, and even though we can't change what happened, we can change how we feel about what happened!

Some things you will have no control over. You can't control stopping a nation going to war, you can't control the outcome of over three million people dying in the next twelve months and you can't control the time you or any of your loved ones will live for. That is up to something far greater than you or me!

We can't walk on the surface of the Sun (like Superhero Dr Manhattan out of the movie Watchmen), nor can we breathe on the surface of Mars without the proper space suit and breathing aids.

However, there are many things that we still can do, and we still need to ask the all-important questions:

"What if?

And

"How can we?"

The reason I brought up Mars is that it seems it's just a

matter of time before people physically set foot on Mars.

There will be many failures along the way, but that's the way life is, failure is never final until you say it is!

So, let's say you've continually failed in mastering your mental state and you keep living in the past and dwelling on regretful moments.

You realise that nothing good will come of you staying this way, you probably already know that, so why are you still doing it?

For many people it's become a habit, just like smoking, just like excessive drinking and just like overeating.

The most important thing you need to do is change! Many people blame it on something else, as if it's outside of their control. Why do they do this?

Most of the time it's because it takes more effort than they are willing to put in, and they get into a state in which they feel comfortable wallowing in self-pity.

It goes back to the old story of a guy walking past a house where there was a dog lying on the porch, in a state of some discomfort.

The man walking past the house could see the elderly owner of the dog sitting in a rocking chair alongside the dog, so he asked, "Why is your dog whimpering?"

The elderly man said, "because he's lying on a nail!"

Puzzled by this, the man said, "Why doesn't he get off the nail?"

Rocking back and forth in his chair, the old man smiled and said, "Because he doesn't want to move!"

The dog didn't want to put in the effort to change things. He felt more comfortable lying on the nail, even though it was unpleasant.

You can either complain about your situation or you can do something about it.

We can make excuses, or get up, make a change, and create a better life for ourselves and the people we care about.

If you're replaying bad things in your mind, then find someone who has had a similar challenge and has overcome what you've been through; learn how they did it. If someone else has overcome it, then so can you!

Never think your struggles are the greatest in the world because I can guarantee you they're not. There are people out there who have been through more hardships than me or you, and they have come out the other side victorious. So, what's the point in ruining your life?

Feed your mind with the positive!

There's a story about an old Cherokee teaching his grandson about life:

The wise old Cherokee said to his grandson:

"A fight is going on inside me. It is a terrible fight between two wolves. One is evil, anger, envy, sorrow, regret, greed, arrogance, self pity, guilt, resentment, inferiority, lies, false pride, superiority, and ego. The other is good, joy, peace, love, hope, serenity, humility, kindness, benevolence, empathy, generosity, truth, compassion, and faith."

The wise old Cherokee continued and told his grandson:

"The same fight is going on inside you and inside every other person too!"

The grandson thought about it for a minute and then asked his grandfather, "Which wolf will win?"

The wise old Cherokee replied, "The one you feed!"

CHAPTER 5

PUSH THROUGH DOUBT AND FEAR

"Inaction breeds doubt and fear. Action breeds confidence and courage. If you want to conquer fear, do not sit at home and think about it. Get busy."
– Dale Carnegie

On the 5th May 1988 in Tottenham, London, a baby girl was born.

Her father and mother split up when she was only a toddler; her father stayed in touch for many years but sadly turned to drink later on in life, which put a strain on their relationship.

However, her mother brought her up with little financially, but she knew her Mum loved her and the young girl had one big dream. That dream was to be a singer!

Her Mum supported her dream, but unlike many successful people's parents, her mum didn't push her into getting a financial backup plan and just encouraged her singing.

She grew up obsessed with pop stars, such as the Spice Girls, Pink, The Backstreet Boys and Britney Spears.

In her teens, she started listening to Destiny's Child, Faith

Evans, Lauren Hill, and P. Diddy; she also loved songs from Ella Fitzgerald, Aretha Franklin, and other successful singers from different eras.

One day she was on a shopping trip to an HMV music shop and was looking through the jazz section. She saw an album cover and liked the hair of one artist she'd never heard of before; it was Etta James, who then became her favourite artist.

When she listened to Etta's sincere singing style the young girl believed every word that Etta sang!

She said that when she started analysing Etta's voice it changed her style of singing from a generic one to a style more like Etta's, but at the same time, allowing her to be true to herself and really going for it when she sang.

The songs she mostly sang about reflected her personal heartbreak, so she put a lot of feeling into them; people heard her songs, and they connected with them on a deeper level! They had been through many of the things she was singing about and could relate to the feeling in her voice.

She got into the BRIT School for Performing Arts and Technology, wrote her own songs and music, and graduated in 2006. Little did she know, that two of her classmates would establish successful careers in the music industry; their names were Amy Winehouse and Jessie J.

Despite being a graduate of the BRIT School, she still suffered from stage fright, but she pushed through her fears, went on stage, and sang her heart out!

She felt pleased for her friends' success, and even though she went to the same performing arts school as them, she had doubts as to whether she could be successful too. However, she focused and kept on pushing towards her dreams!

Relentless in her quest for success, she published two songs into the online Art Publication Platforms Magazine and also did a class project that included a three-song demo, which her friend posted on a new social media network called MySpace; amazingly, that post lead to a phone call from the boss of the Indie (independent) music label XL Recordings; XL wasn't a huge label, but they were very professional and had a lot of credibility. Some of their acts included The Prodigy, Radiohead and Dizzy Rascal.

After signing for XL, she went straight into the recording studio and captured several songs she had already written.

However, the surrounding buzz had gathered momentum, and the esteemed pianist, bandleader, singer, composer, and TV presenter Jools Holland wanted her on his 'Later… with Jools Holland' show on the BBC.

So, before XL had released one of her singles, she was already making headlines on the TV!

Her first album didn't break the top 50 in the United States, but determined to make it in America, she set up a tour there.

One break she got in America was performing on the hit TV show 'Saturday Night Live.'

At the same time presidential candidate Sarah Palin was on the show. This helped her receive massive viewing figures and led to her current single shooting up in the US charts and her album getting into the US Top 10.

That's how powerful marketing and getting in front of an audience can be!

She didn't expect the sudden attention, but later confessed that she had her doubts and fears, saying that she mentally beat herself up too much.

This is something that most of us will do in our lives, but

the good news is that we can all overcome it!

One person talking about her said: "She has no image, she's not glamorous, but people are buying her single because her song is connecting with them in a very special way and is beautifully sung."

Most of the time she didn't have lots of backing dancers, she didn't have flashing lights all over the place, she didn't have people jumping out of cakes and swinging around on trapeze; it was just her on stage, sometimes with just a guitar, and sometimes all on her own with a microphone.

If you were a betting man (or betting woman) back then, you would never have believed that this old school music that she was singing would be such a hit with the younger generation, but a hit it was!

Her debut album launched in 2008, the sales went eight-times platinum in the United Kingdom (just one time platinum being the equivalent to 300,000 albums sold in the United Kingdom); and three-times platinum in the United States (just one time platinum being the equivalent to 1,000,000 sales in the United States).

In the 51st Grammy Awards in 2009, she received the awards for Best New Artist and Best Female Pop Vocal

Performance; her name is 'Adele Laurie Blue Adkins,' aka 'Adele'!

For her third single, Adele joined up with successful producer Mark Ronson, but despite collaborating with such a successful producer, the song struggled to reach the top 20 in the UK.

Adele mainly liked to sing her own songs, but there was a Bob Dylan song she came across that she really loved. At the same time, Adele said she was overly critical of herself because she didn't know if she could do the original short song justice.

Despite her doubts, she pushed through her fears, picked herself up and the song was a tremendous hit!

No matter how successful you get, there will always be challenges along the way, and when Adele had to perform at the Grammy Awards in 2016, there was a strange clanging noise coming from the piano, which everybody in the audience and at home watching on TV could hear. If this wasn't off-putting enough, while she was singing her microphone was malfunctioning.

Adele soldiered on and got a standing ovation from the audience!

That same year, Adele was singing at the Birmingham NEC when the audio cut off again. However, this time, the entire crowd filled in the silence, as they knew the words... it was brilliant!

The following year again at the Grammy Awards, Adele had more technical difficulties, but like the winner she is, she came through and stole the show!

Even though she has appeared on stage many times, Adele admitted on the Ellen DeGeneres Show that she still has stage fright and feels that because of her success, she feels even more pressure to perform well.

In 2011, 2012 and 2016, Billboard named Adele 'The Artist of The Year' and she listed at number 5 on VH1 100 Greatest Women in Music in 2012.

At only 24 years of age, Adele became one of the highest selling artists of all time, and in 2012 and 2016 Time Magazine named her one of the most influential women in the world!

Adele's 2016 to 2017 tour, broke attendance records in several countries including the UK, Australia and the United States and has now sold over 100 million records.

When people discovered the song 'Hello,' Adele's website

was getting over 4,000 hits a second!

However, even after the success of Adele's first two albums, she went through doubts and a stage where she didn't believe in herself.

When Adele rocked up to an interview on CBS' news magazine 60 Minutes, she said never in a million years did she think this would happen to her.

So, you would think that with all of this incredible success Adele breezes through life. However, no matter how successful you get, whether it's public or in a less public way, there are still many challenges to face!

Adele admits to feeling scared just before she releases a new album, as she cares about her fans and doesn't want to disappoint them.

She felt fearful about going on stage, but she battled through and overcame it, which was to the benefit of not only her, but millions of people around the world!

Sometimes, facing your fears can be the best thing you can do because it stretches you and you grow from it mentally; not only that, you can help so many other people.

One thing I love the most about Adele is her down-to-earth attitude. She hasn't let fame or riches go to her head and deep down inside, she is still just that friendly girl from North London.

Here are some lessons we can learn from Adele's story. The chances are you can find even more lessons in her story for yourself that will be helpful to you:

- Just because you have doubts sometimes, it doesn't mean you can't achieve great things.

- Do what you love.

- Find inspiration from other people.

- Put your heart and soul into it.

- Make a beeline to get all of the best contacts and connections.

- Face your fears.

- Keep going even when things go wrong.

- Stay grounded and down-to-earth.

CHAPTER 6

SUCK IT UP

"An inventor fails 999 times, and if he succeeds once, he is in.
He treats his failure as practice shots."
– Charles F. Kettering

In October 2017, I was slightly frustrated and feeling slightly overwhelmed that I hadn't done enough to get my next few books out.

I was also torn between spending time with my son Léon, having some time to myself, working for immediate cash to put food on the table and paying bills, whilst also putting time into my author career.

One evening, I sat down and watched several episodes of 'Shark Tank,' the US reality TV show where entrepreneurs pitch their inventions and business ideas to wealthy investors.

It's a show that I really enjoy watching because it shows people with a dream, who have put a lot of dedication into their company or product, and want to see it to go from success to success!

One week earlier, I was on holiday in Monaco, the South

of France and Italy.

While I was in Monaco, I needed to use a public toilet, so I walked into one just below Prince Albert's Palace, on one of the main streets, and I noticed that I was drying my hands with a Dyson Airblade hand dryer.

I'd been thinking about writing about James Dyson and the success story of his vacuum cleaners and hand dryers, which led me to write these words. Sometimes in life, it's as if you're shown a path to follow.

James Dyson thought most vacuum cleaners suck (excuse the pun).

When James Dyson was using his vacuum cleaner one day, he noticed that the cleaner was losing suction power. He got angry and took the machine apart, so that he could understand it, and see what the problem was.

He first thought that the dust got deposited into the bag and that the suction depended on the power output of the motor.

When he took the machine apart, he realised that the dust travelled into the bag, and the air went with it through the bag. Subsequently, the bag's pores become clogged with the dust in the bag, which then cuts down the airflow, reducing the level of suction as a result.

James went to a lumbar yard and saw a cyclone on the roof, which collected dust off of the saws and planers and soon realised that the cyclone wasn't clogging up and blocking the airflow. Instead, it was spinning the sawdust out of the air stream and the clean air was going out of a chimney at the top.

James wondered why that cyclone system wasn't used for collecting dust inside vacuum cleaners.

He rushed home and built a cyclone out of cardboard and gaffer tape (as you do). He then inserted this into an upright vacuum cleaner and astonishingly, it worked! From that day on, James Dyson devoted his life to making the best vacuum cleaner.

Even though his initial prototype appeared to work, it still needed a lot of improvement. Dyson wanted to partner with existing vacuum cleaner manufacturers, but the manufacturers were unwilling to disrupt the hundred million pound vacuum bag market. Due to this, the last thing that they wanted to hear about was a bagless vacuum cleaner.

James thought it would take around 6 months before he got it right, but it took him 4 – 5 years!

By 1992, James had been working on the project for over four years.

Even though he was borrowing money from the bank, he ran out of money.

He went to all the venture capitalists, but they rejected him.

Eventually, a bank agreed to lend him the money with the condition that it was secured on his house.

When he tried to get his vacuum cleaner into the shops, most of the retailers told him that they didn't know who he was, and he had no brand name; so on that basis they rejected him.

However, through determination and persistence, he got some retailers to take a chance on his vacuum cleaner and it started selling. However, even when he got his new vacuum cleaner on sale, as cool and as beautiful as this new vacuum cleaner looked, and as great a product as it was, many people said it was far too expensive, and no one would buy it; it was three times the price of the average vacuum cleaner!

However, people tried it, liked it and the rest as they say is history!

Sure, the Dyson brand is world famous now, but inbetween 1979 and 1984 Dyson tested 5,127 prototype cyclone vacuum cleaners before he getting it right!

Let me say that number again so it just sinks in... 5,127!

That's 5,127 times before he perfected his bagless vacuum cleaner.

Now, that's what you call being relentless and never giving in!

However, James Dyson is far from the stereotypical inventor that we think of. He's not in a little shed, working on genius ideas (at least not now at the time of writing he's not.) James Dyson knows that to make his products succeed on a larger scale he has to surround himself with hundreds of scientists, mathematicians, engineers, and a great marketing team.

He couldn't do it all on his own!

Dyson confessed that he was a terrible student in school, and when he started his quest to invent a bagless vacuum cleaner, many people told him that it was a mad idea and that he would definitely go bankrupt!

He said:

"The problem with wanting to develop new technology and trying to do something in a vastly different way is that it's never worked before. Failure is the wonderful starting point because when something fails you've got to think and experiment to overcome that failure; you always realise that there must be something better around the corner. Only one day in 100 will you break through and make a success of it and provide something that was never done before... that's what's incredibly exciting! The whole point about inventing is that because it's not easy and what you're doing is impossible, no one has managed to do it before. Just build prototypes, keep testing, and never give up!"

Here are some things that we can learn from the James Dyson story:

- You don't need to be brilliant at school to succeed in life.

- Look for lessons in life each day that you can learn from (just as the cyclone in the sawmill taught James Dyson).

- You will always get people telling you, "It can't be done."

- Don't be discouraged by critics, use them to motivate you.

- It's natural to fail before you succeed.

- Interpret failures as success and a step towards where you need to go.

- Get a great team around you.

- To succeed massively, be willing to fail massively.

- Your dream may take longer to be achieved than you first thought.

- Keep going and never give in.

"I look at things and wonder if they could be made better and start thinking about how they are made and that's what interests me."
– James Dyson

CHAPTER 7

HELP OTHER PEOPLE

"No one is useless in this world who lightens the burdens of another."
– Charles Dickens

I remember one day driving along and seeing a guy pulling a cart with a tall flag on the back. He was doing a charity walk, so I pulled over and had a chat with him.

His name was Darren Greenhalgh, and he was doing a walk around England and Wales for Combat Stress, a charity that helps ex forces people who are dealing with post-traumatic stress disorder (PTSD).

I asked Darren if he would let me interview him and he agreed.

The next challenge was to find a suitable place where we could do an interview, so I went over to a place called the Silverdale Lodge, which is in a small village called Johnston, and they agreed to let us do it.

"If you don't ask, you don't get."

I asked Darren if he had contacted the local media about

his trek to which he replied no, so I immediately got on the phone and contacted the local media for him. So many times we wait to do something, and that time can be lost forever if we don't seize the moment.

Tony Robbins has many quotes cited to him, but I love this one,

"Never set a goal without putting in some action towards achieving that goal!"

That way you are already moving forward, and you'll feel a great deal of satisfaction when you've done something about your goal, especially if it's towards helping other people!

Darren told me he couldn't believe there are people like me out there, "What do you mean?" I said.

Darren said that the day before I met him, he had had enough, and had thoughts of giving up! He was missing his children, and he questioned if anyone cared about what he was doing.

Sometimes life can be like this, especially if you have your heart set on doing something that you believe can make a difference in people's lives.

There will be times when what you're doing seems pointless and not worthwhile.

However, if you feel that you have a mission in life, then hold on and keep going because help can be just around the corner!

Many people give up way too soon; the reason that achievements are 'achievements' is because they're not everyday routine tasks that are easy.

What makes your achievement worthwhile is that you've put effort into it, you've completed what you set out to do and you've probably inspired other people along the way!

There were many things achieved by stopping and talking to Darren that day

1. It lifted his spirits.

2. It raised more awareness and money for his great cause, 'Combat Stress.'

3. I had created another interview with someone who was achieving great things.

4. It inspired me and many other people who saw what Darren was doing to help others.

While talking to me, Darren mentioned things other people had achieved, and said what he was doing was nothing compared to what they had. But the reality was, Darren was doing something significant! What Darren was doing hasn't been achieved by even 1% of the population, which is awesome!

We can all look at other people and say, "It's nothing compared to what he or she achieved", but we need to take a moment and think about how far we have come. What other people achieve can be great and inspiring, but don't put yourself down by comparing yourself with what others have done. As long as you're moving forward and making progress yourself, that's all that matters!

I was about to say goodbye to Darren when walking to my car I thought, "No, I'd like to walk with him up the road for a bit." It was great to see that people were beeping their horns and showing support for what Darren was doing.

While walking up the road, we bumped into former British and Welsh rugby league player Jonathan Griffiths.

Johnny also agreed to do an interview; It's amazing what comes your way when you stop to help people and add some value to their lives. Sometimes we wait about too long for things to be perfect, but perfection doesn't exist because there is always something more that you can add to make things better.

One of the big mistakes that many people make, is that they don't help others enough.

Many people that are going through a tough time stop thinking about others. However, if you're going through a tough time, then it can be a good thing to take the focus off of yourself and help other people.

You are far stronger mentally than you probably give yourself credit for, and there are hundreds, if not thousands, of people out there that will need your help!

You may think to yourself that you don't know thousands of people. But if you can help five people, those five people can help five other people, which can lead to them helping five other people and eventually, through your small actions, you could affect thousands of people in a positive way!

Some people don't like to help others because they get jealous of other people's success. This can stem from fear, which may cause you to think, "Hey if I help this person too much, then they may become more successful than me and leave me behind."

However, if you genuinely want to help somebody, you should be happy for their success, because their success is your success even if you don't get the credit.

I touch on the importance of surrounding yourself with the right people in some of my books because it's fundamental to being a happier and more positive person.

The saying that goes, "It's about who you know" is true, but you still have to make things happen yourself. However, if you want to create bigger things for yourself and the people around you, then it's a good idea to be humble enough to realise that you'll need a helping hand along the way.

Sure, we must make it happen by putting ourselves out there, but as the other saying goes, "No man or woman is an island." As you connect more and more with positive people, you'll start to enjoy life more.

Sure, there are people out there who aren't as genuine as they first appear to be. There are people out there who are only in it for themselves and will trample over you if they think that they'll benefit from that. But that behaviour is short lived for those people, and eventually what they send out into the universe will come back to them!

As you move up the ladder with contacts, you'll be able to

do more for people you care about, and you'll be able to help your friends, who also want to achieve big things. It's awesome when you help other people, and if they're nice people, they'll be very thankful to you for helping.

It all goes in a circle; you make them happy and they make you happy. It's a win-win for everyone!

Sometimes, you can help people and still be struggling through life. However, keep helping people because at some point things will come back to you, and you'll get that lucky break!

For years I held back on pushing the knowledge I have that can help so many people, but I found that once I got more of my positive messages out through newspapers, radio, social media and now books, my life changed for the better.

If you have knowledge that can help people, then why keep it to yourself?

Sometimes people have all this knowledge that can help thousands or millions of people, but they don't push it out into the world. This can be due to fear, or because they don't think that what they have will be of any use to people.

That's one challenge many of us face (including me at one point). We sell ourselves short and think, "Hey, why would anyone be interested in what I've got to say."

But keeping your knowledge, skills, and abilities to yourself does no one any good, including yourself!

And these days with social media, it's even easier than ever. These days all you need to do is post something on Facebook, Snapchat, LinkedIn, Twitter, YouTube, or whatever platform it is, to get yourself out there to the world. At first it can be just a few positive words to get you out there in cyberspace, then you can post photos and when you gain even more confidence, you can post videos about what value you can bring to people.

But if you're just going to moan to people all the time, many people will eventually tire of you acting the victim and lose interest in you.

Having a website is a great thing to have. If you're going to be selling things, then you also must look into online marketing tools such as Aweber, MailChimp and Infusionsoft to send automated emails to people with valuable offers and services that you can provide for them.

I never really liked sales, in some weird way I used to look at it as uncool, but the truth is we all have to sell ourselves whether it's to a sponsor, an employer, a partner or anything else.

We need to tell people why we're the best person for that position; we need to show people what skills and value we can bring to them or their company. That's not being big-headed, that's more about having belief in yourself and knowing that you're worthy of the position.

For me, one of the major benefits of helping others is that it makes me feel better about myself. So, by sending out good vibes to people, the chances are they'll come back.

Sure you can be the nicest person in the world and some people can treat you like a piece of shit, but the more good vibes you send out to people, the more good vibes come back to you!

So, go out there and help others and it will help you too!

CHAPTER 8

FAILURE AND FAIRYTALES

"All my troubles and obstacles have strengthened me. You may not realise this when it happens, but a kick in the teeth may be the best thing for you."
– Walt Disney

Get Back Up

Don Hahn grew up loving Disney animation movies.

He loved Disney animation movies so much that when he was 20 years old, he got a job at Disney delivering artwork and coffee to the animators at the Disney studios.

Delivering artwork and making coffee for the animators may not sound like the most glorious job in the world, but Don himself says he felt like he'd won the lottery, as he was amongst the people whom he respected. We'll come back to Don's story a little later in this chapter.

The Disney documentary 'Waking Sleeping Beauty,' talks about the rollercoaster of a ride that the animators went through while trying to make cartoon movies. In the 1980s, Disney animation was struggling and produced a series of movies that were failures.

On the outside, if somebody would've told you that they were working at the Disney animation studios, it would've got a lot of kudos, but behind-the-scenes there was a tremendous amount of pressure for the Disney animation team to perform. Now, Disney is renowned for making outstanding animation movies!

However, in the 1970s and the 1980s, Disney animation went through a massive slump and was declining in popularity. A survey of a group of teenagers revealed that they wouldn't be seen dead going to a Disney animated movie! It was a far cry from the glory days of 'Snow White and The Seven Dwarfs!'

During this big slump, the Disney board of directors made a major decision and brought in new leadership, hoping they would change Disney animation around. Michael Eisner became their new Chairman, and Frank Wells became their Chief Operating Officer.

Disney had come up with an animation called 'The Black Cauldron,' which was a very dark movie. It cost around $40 million to make and it bombed at the box office, taking only half of what it cost to make in ticket sales.

The producers of 'The Black Cauldron' thought that it would do well, but it got beat by 'The Care Bear Movie,' which didn't go down well at Disney. After this disappointment, the Disney animation team got back up and tried again.

They brought a theatrical and film producer called Peter Sneijder into the animation studios to head up the division. Peter strongly believed in encouraging his animators and empowering them to achieve their goals. He said that he wanted the entire team to feel good about themselves and to value their work as world class.

Peter also brought in the NBA Lakers basketball coach Pat Riley to give motivational talks. He also encouraged his animators to be hypercritical about anything, in the hope that it would make things better.

The design studio produced hundreds, if not thousands, of concept drawings that often got binned, but they got back up and carried on and believed they could make great animation. This would be discouraging to some people, but they carried on regardless!

Anyone at Disney could have an idea for a movie title. Whether it was a caretaker, a secretary, or a delivery person. Anyone!

The people at Disney didn't just think about new ideas, they thought about old ideas that were never acted on.

After years of disappointment and failure, the team had a breakthrough when they came up with the movie 'The Little Mermaid.'

'The Little Mermaid' lifted the Disney animation studios out of the dark depths of failure, and it soared to global success! However, just because you're at the top, it doesn't mean that you will stay at the top. After the success of 'The Little Mermaid,' Disney animation was struggling to make another big hit movie.

They invested in new computer animation technology to make things better and made a movie which they called 'Rescuers Down Under.' It didn't have a great reception, and the marketing was cut from it.

This was heartbreaking for many of the animators and the rest of the team that had worked so hard on the project!

Walt Disney himself had come up with an idea for a movie in the 1940s, but it got shelved at the time and never came to fruition during his lifetime. However, the Disney team decided that they now wanted to make the movie, even though so many people had rejected the idea before. They cut the schedule and budget for this next movie back from previous movies, and Disney bosses recruited two young story artists, Gary Trousdale and Kirk Wise, to become the movie's directors, as the previous director dropped out.

There was a lot of in-house disagreement at Disney about the suggestion that this animated movie should become a musical animation, but a musical animation it became.

It gained widespread critical acclaim and won the Golden Globe award for 'Best Motion Picture – Musical,' which made it the first animated film to win in this category!

It also became the first animated movie to be nominated for Best Picture Award at the Academy Awards, where it won the Academy Award for Best Original Score and Best Original Song. That French fairytale movie had a budget of only $25 million and took a box office of $440 million!

The movie shelved for over 40 years got back up and became one of the biggest box office smashes in animation history. They called the movie… 'Beauty and the Beast.'

'Aladdin' followed, and it became the highest grossing film of 1992 and earned over $504 million at the box office.

The animation studio, once considered the weak link of the Disney Empire, had now become a respected and dominant force! Animation was now not only for children, but adults also loved it!

The characters born out of peoples imaginations, drawn on storyboards, and later made into movies, also became new characters in the Disney parks.

Disney then started working on an animation which the team called, 'Bambi in Africa.' The animators were not excited about 'Bambi in Africa,' because the buzz was about a new movie they were bringing out called 'Pocahontas.' Most animators didn't want to work on this silly 'Bambi in Africa' story.

But before we talk about that, let's find out what happened to Don Hahn, the young 20-year-old that was the delivery boy and coffee maker for the Disney animators.

Through determination, belief in himself, the ability to work well with people, and the resilience to get back up when he failed, Don produced that little French fairytale they called 'Beauty and the Beast.' Don also produced that movie most people didn't want to work on, which the Disney team nicknamed 'Bambi in Africa.'

Despite the lack of interest in 'Bambi in Africa,' Don and his team made the movie.

It was later called 'The Lion King!'

The budget for 'The Lion King' was $45 million, and it took a staggering $968 million at the box office!

It became the highest grossing release of 1994 and the

highest grossing animated film of all time! It also became the second highest grossing film, and the best-selling film on home video. It won many awards and became a phenomenon as a theatre production too!

The Disney team experienced doubt, fear, failures, and many negative challenges, but they got back up and never gave in!

And if they can get back up… so can you!

CHAPTER 9

LIFE IS LIKE THE SEASONS

"You must take personal responsibility. You cannot change the circumstances, the seasons, or the wind, but you can change yourself."
– Jim Rohn

We all have our own spring, summer, autumn, and winter during our lives.

The spring being the good times in our life, the summer being the bright and fantastic times in our life, the autumn being the slightly challenging times in our life, and the winter is the darker and tougher times in our life.

Many people think to themselves that if one problem in their life is fixed, then everything will be ok. However, life has a habit of always throwing challenges our way!

Many people think that when they have more money they'll feel happy, or when they achieve a certain goal they'll feel happy, or when they have the right partner they'll feel happy, or when they end their relationship they'll feel happy, or if they change their job, they'll feel happy.

Changing certain circumstances can improve the quality

of your life, but it's also important to enjoy the present because that is what we live everyday!

Sometimes, we can beat ourselves up for not being in the position we want to be in life.

We may not get enough time off and freedom from our work.

We may not have the perfect relationship.

We may be in a relationship but want the freedom of being single.

We may not have the dream house we want, or the fancy cars, or the clothes we want.

Maybe the father or mother of our children is causing problems.

Maybe we don't have the exotic holidays that we want every year.

Most of us will have these thoughts at some point, and the important thing is not to dwell on this too much or look into the past and think about what you have lost. If you always focus on what you haven't got, your situation will not improve.

If whatever you once had in your life has now gone, the only thing you can do now is move forward! It doesn't mean that you can forget about your loss, especially if it's the loss of a loved one. But you must get back up. Not only for others that need you, but for yourself!

Change is the only thing in this world that is constant, and whether we like it or not, we must adapt to it!

A few years ago, I was running around a place, called the racecourse, in my hometown of Haverfordwest when I felt sad at my lack of achievements. I was not in a good place financially, I had lost my job, the beautiful house I was staying in, I was deeply in debt and was finding it challenging to make ends meet.

While running around, I was thinking about all I had lost and how difficult it had become to make my dreams come true. As I kept on running, I realised what I was doing, I was telling myself about all the of things that weren't going right for me and I was focusing on them.

If I were to still focus on these things, I would never have got out of that situation and never have made my dreams come true. While thinking about how I had so called 'failed in life,' I had forgotten about all of the amazing things that I had done and achieved in my life. I started thinking to myself, "Hey, stop your bitching, and check out what you have got and done!"

After coming out of school, I had gone to Europe to represent the national team in Tug of War.

Against all odds, I had become an Army Commando, a Bodyguard, a Personal Trainer, completed my skydiving and scuba diving courses, flown a plane, ran in the Sahara, ran across the USA, broke a running world record, traveled to Venice, Paris, Rome, Cancun, Las Vegas and through California. I had been to 9 different States in the United States and travelled to over 50 countries around the world. But most importantly, I have got a perfect little boy.

I was in great shape, had very good health and was also living in an outstanding country. This list goes on and on, so should I have really been thinking about how shit my life was? Should I have been thinking about how much of a loser I was, just because of a few setbacks?

I shouldn't have, and neither should you!

Think about all of the things that you've done in your life. Don't compare them to anyone else's life, just focus on some of the things that you've done, that at one point in time, were just a dream.

Zig Ziglar hits the nail on the head when he says,

"Failure isn't a person, it's just an event."

Just because you've failed lots of times before doesn't mean that you will continue to fail throughout the rest of your life. When you fail lots of times at something, it can take the wind out of your sails. But, that's what happens to everyone who strives to achieve goals!

Many of the best athletes who you see on the TV and read about have suffered injuries and setbacks on their road to success. It's not all plain sailing. They will go through many of the things that a normal person will go through (money challenges, relationship break ups, loved one's dying) but they get back on track and focus on their goals again!

If you're not feeling good about yourself, then you need to take a check of the situation and see what you've already got. Chances are, you've done a lot with your life and if you haven't, then it's never too late to start great things!

Write a list down and see what is good in your life.

Even superstars have challenges in life. I remember a journalist interviewing Brad Pitt one day and saying something like "Your life is so great; do you ever have bad days where you're not happy?"

Brad replied,

"I do. I have good days, and not so good days."

And if someone has 6 children, you can bet your ass that there are some tough days and challenges!

This is just the way life is, it's tough, it's challenging, and you'd better get a grip and get used to it! No matter what you have, do, and achieve, there will always be challenges ahead.

Elon Musk has an estimated net worth of billions of dollars, but guess what, he still has financial challenges! He's struggled many times in business, and it's caused some stress and upset over the years. What this goes to show is that, no matter what your financial situation, you will still face many challenges.

Ok, so you may be trying to put food on the table, put fuel in your car and keep up the payment for the phone and house etc, which is different to finding funds for Elon's next space rocket. However, most people stress and worry at some point, and these are things we must overcome!

If you're going through a challenging time at the moment,

or in the future, just know that life is like the seasons. We're all going to have springs, summers, autumns and winters in our life, and it's important to remember that you can, and will, see happier times ahead when you face the winters of your life!

When you're going through these dark times, get back up because there are good times ahead!

"Never give up, for that is just a place and time that the tide will turn."
– Harriet Beecher Stowe

CHAPTER 10

MY LOAD IS HEAVIER THAN YOURS

"This above all, refuse to be a victim."
– Margaret Atwood

I know quite a bit of this book is focused on achieving your goals and how attaining them can give you a higher sense of self-worth. However, reaching your goals isn't the primary key to your happiness. No matter how many things you achieve, whether it be fitness, sports, money, education, or anything else, if you constantly focus on the bad things in your life or the things you haven't got, your life will be shit!

I was once criticised by someone who resented me for being happy and achieving many of my dreams, so that person told everyone that life isn't that easy and sometimes life can be hard.

It's true that life will be challenging for us, but because an event happened to us one, two, five or ten years ago, it doesn't mean you must replay how bad you feel about it every single day!

The critic played the song of;

"My life is tougher than yours and my load is heavier than yours!"

Everywhere that person went, they would tell other people about this thing that happened in the past and was continuously banging on about it on social media for everyone to see.

I'm not saying that you shouldn't have some sympathy for people who have had a challenging time, but when you hear the same negative thing again and again and again, it wears a little thin!

If you harp on about something that happened in the past, whether it was someone cheating on you, a loved one passing, losing your job, going on about how tough things are, people soon tire of hearing it. If you've been through a challenging or heart-breaking time, then yes it can be tough, but realise you're in the same boat as billions of other people!

If someone like Oprah who was abused as a child can overcome that or people who have had acid thrown in their face and suffered horrendous life changing burns can live a great life, then so can you!

If somebody ends up a quadriplegic and can go on to live a fulfilling life, so can you!

If Viktor Frankl can overcome his family being murdered in the Nazi death camps, then you too can overcome what has happened in your life!

The biggest mistake that people make when they are struggling with overcoming something, is that they repeatedly focus on their suffering. They wake up the next day, continue the same mental process and think the same thoughts as they did the day before.

Einstein said that,

"The definition of insanity is doing the same thing again and again and expecting different results."

If you want to win, you have to expect to win and live the good life.

Some people call this arrogance, and maybe it is to a certain extent, but there are two types of arrogance: the first is when you think that you're the most important person in the world and everyone else is beneath you, and the second is when you have total belief and confidence in yourself.

The second is by far the better type of arrogance (if people want to call it that), and if you can match confidence and belief in yourself with having respect for other people and have a sense of humility, then you've pretty much cracked it!

You sometimes see people that have constant dramas going on in their life; part of that can be that they are trying to make themselves look more important, and they want to get more attention from other people. Many of these drama type people don't realise that their anger and arguing has become a way of life, and that's all they know.

Some people will say, 'you can't teach an old dog new tricks,' but you can teach a dog a new trick. However, you can only teach a dog new tricks if the dog (or human) takes on board the information and applies the new tricks to their lives.

If you're going through a very challenging time, it may be difficult for you to see yourself living a happy and fulfilling life. You may think that there is no way out of the situation and that those dark days are here to stay, but there's always a way out!

Many people get stuck in a rut and can't seem to make things better for themselves.

They think that people who are happy and make their dreams come true are just lucky, and that the laws of fate just smile on these people from the day they were born!

But when you look at happy, high achieving people, there are things that have gone on in their lives that have rocked them to the core at some point! It doesn't matter how tough you are, life at some point will make you doubt yourself; it will make you doubt the outcome of things.

The good news is that it is a natural thing of life, and most, if not all humans will experience it.

So, if the vast majority of people go through this, and can get through it, so can you!

"When you complain, you make yourself a victim.
Leave the situation, change the situation, or accept it.
All else is madness."
– Eckhart Tolle

CHAPTER 11

VANILLA ICE ICE BABY

"It is not the critic who counts; not the man who points out how the strongman stumbles, or where the doer of deeds could have done better. The credit belongs to the man who is actually in the arena, whose face is marred by dust and sweat and blood; who strives valiantly; who errs, who comes short again, and again, because there is no effort without error and shortcoming; but who does actually strive to do the deeds; who knows the great enthusiasms, the great devotions; who spends himself in a worthy cause; who at best knows in the end the triumph of high achievement, and who at worst, if he fails, at least fails while daring greatly, so that his place shall never be with those cold and timid souls who neither know victory nor defeat."
– Theodore Roosevelt

Two school friends both wanted to be 'someone' in life, but they were far from being the popular kids in school; in fact, they were the nerdy kids that were looked on by many as uncool!

When they left school, they grew beards and went from one dead-end job to another. Many people would class them as two hippy losers that weren't going anywhere in the world. They were fed up with doing jobs they found unsatisfying and wanted to do something that they thought they may enjoy; so in 1977, they thought about setting up a food business.

After much thought, they filtered their options down to two niche food types: bagels or ice cream. When they priced up how much it would cost to start up a bagel business, it turned out that it was far too expensive for their limited funds.

However, the ice cream business was within their budget

range. Unfortunately, they had no idea about ice cream or about business. So, they sent off for a $5 course on owning and operating an ice cream business. If you were a gambler, you would have probably bet against these two dreamers having ever made their business into a success story.

They looked all over for a location for their first ice cream store and eventually set up in an abandoned petrol station in Burlington, Vermont.

The guys were looked upon as these two local hippies, but the community was supportive of them and their ice cream was liked, so the store got off to a good start and soon became popular.

It was different to most ice cream shops, with their focus on a quirky and fun customer experience. They thought outside of the box with the wacky, but tasty recipes for their ice creams and regular entertainment acts, such as a blues singer and pianist.

But one of the major reasons that people loved going to the shop was the warm and engaging personalities of the two owners, as they were an experience in themselves.

Although the store was doing substantial business in the summer, it became a different story in the winter, as the demand for ice cream dropped. The two owners knew that if they didn't diversify, the business would not survive the seasonal downturn. So they started selling their uniquely flavoured ice cream to local restaurants within the city of Burlington, using an old truck to deliver the goods.

Although not every restaurant agreed to stock it, some did, which helped with their diminished cash flow. However the truck was unreliable, and it was costing them more with repairs than the profits they were making from selling the ice cream.

This was now a crisis for the duo, as they had virtually no money left in their business!

They knew that they had a great product that was liked by the people, and they also loved their home state of Vermont, but they knew that they had to sell to other states too to survive.

While attempting to sell their ice cream to supermarkets, they found that it wasn't the done thing to sell from the back of a pickup truck. Large stores use distributors to get their products, so they had to get a leading distributor onboard.

One of them drove to the distributor's office and got there

at 4 o'clock in the morning. He couldn't afford a hotel and stayed in his car; of course, this isn't the most comfortable place to sleep, but it was even less comfortable when the car froze over during the night! However, he was willing to do whatever it took to see the distributor, even if it meant driving miles out of his way, sleeping in his car and half freezing to death!

When it came to the appointment time, he walked into the distributor's office looking dishevelled. Of course, this isn't the normal way people conduct business, but what he lacked in smart appearance, he made up for in personality and enthusiasm!

The distributor agreed to help them sell their ice cream and with one distributor in the bag, the duo realised that they needed another distributor.

Again, with his next appointment with a different distributor, he went in just wearing a pair of sports shoes and old scruffy clothes. It worked, for a second time. Bingo! They now had their distribution channels to supermarkets.

In 1978, the king of the premium ice cream market was Haagen-Dazs, and no one, but no one stood in their way!

Haagen-Dazs owned a massive 70% of the market!

Even though the two friends still had a very tiny ice cream business compared to Haagen-Dazs, the corporate giant still wanted to crush them before they posed any threat, no matter how insignificant! So, they phoned the distributors and gave them an ultimatum: either stock Haagen-Dazs or stock other ice cream products.

If the distributors carried on wanting to distribute their competitors ice cream, then Haagen-Dazs would cut them off!

This put the distributors in an awkward position, as they were selling enormous amounts of Haagen-Dazs ice cream and small amounts of the new ice cream from the fledgling company owned by the Vermont duo.

This was terrible news to the two friends, as they knew that with Haagen-Dazs putting pressure on the distributors, they would most likely cut them out and use Haagen-Dazs!

Also, if they couldn't use any distributors, then their new ice cream brand was dead in the water! However, the two friends got back up, and decided that they weren't willing to stand back and let their new ice cream business collapse from corporate bullying.

With that in mind, they were willing to fight the big boys!

It was a real David and Goliath story, so in came the lawyers!

They knew that the chances of winning in court against a corporate giant were very slim, but at this point, they felt that they had nothing to lose.

The parent company of Haagen-Dazs – Pillsbury (a multibillion dollar company who also owned Burger King and several other successful businesses) carried a substantial legal clout with 17 lawyers behind them, whereas the two friends had just the one.

The two friends decided, rather than put their focus on fighting Haagen-Dazs, they wanted to fight the larger parent company Pillsbury, as taking on a massive conglomerate would stir up more public support and show that this was more than just two ice cream companies fighting.

Their plan worked, and they achieved an out of court settlement with the added condition that distributors could stock their ice cream alongside Haagen-Dazs without any repercussions.

Unsurprisingly, the tremendous amount of publicity generated by the legal case was something that the duo could not have dreamt or even afforded before, and their brand grew massively!

People loved the bold different flavours, and it fitted with their bold stance against the giants Haagen-Dazs and Pillsbury.

The names of the two friends who started the quirky little ice cream business were Mr Cohen and Mr Greenfield, but you may have heard of their first names... Ben & Jerry.

Ben & Jerry's ice cream went on to become a colossal worldwide success!

However, just because the company went on to be a big success, it didn't mean that everything was plain sailing and that they were successful at everything.

For example, they have had a lot of failures as well as successes with the ice cream flavours.

Some of these failures include:

Sugar Plum, Fossil Fuel, Holy Cannoli, Oh Pear, Rainforest Crunch, Wild Maine Blueberry, Wavy Gravy, Vermont Python, Bovinity Divinity, Tennessee Mud, Purple Passion Fruit, Turtle Soup, Economic Crunch, Miz Jelena's Sweet Potato Pie, Chocolate Peanut Butter Cookie Dough, Peanut Butter and Jelly, Schweddy Balls

Here are some things that we can learn from the Ben & Jerry's story:

- Start with what you've got, even if it's very little.

- Be friendly.

- Don't concern yourself with what people think about you.

- Be willing to take on risks and new challenges.

- If you're doing a job you hate, find something more fulfilling.

- Provide a great product.

- Provide multiple products.

- Be willing to try different things.

- Have a good sense of humour.

- Be willing to travel if your job requires it.

- Think outside the box.

- Have an excellent team around you.

- Risk looking like a fool.

- Be willing to go the extra mile.

- When you need help, don't be afraid to ask for it.

- Be willing to take on enormous challenges.

- Most people will go through financial challenges, but you can turn things around.

- When there are challenges against you, keep going.

- Know that even when you're successful there will be challenges.

- Have a positive attitude.

- Tell yourself that you will succeed.

Who would've ever believed that two friends could start an ice cream business that would turn into an ice cream empire?

Here is a list of some countries where Ben & Jerry's now have locations (at the time of writing).

Aruba, Australia, Austria, Bahamas, Belgium, Brazil, Canada, Croatia, Czech Republic, Denmark, Estonia, Finland, France, Germany, Greece, Ireland, Israel, Italy, Malaysia, Mexico, Netherlands, Netherlands Antilles, New Zealand, Norway, Poland, Portugal, Romania, Serbia, Singapore, Slovakia, Spain, Sweden, Switzerland, Thailand, United Arab Emirates, United Kingdom, United States

Ben and Jerry showed us that by starting small, having a big dream, and being persistent, it will help you to achieve great things with your life.

So, focus on what you really want to achieve and go out there and achieve it!

"Do not judge me by my successes, judge me by how many times I fell down and got back up again."
— Nelson Mandela

CHAPTER 12

SNAP OUT OF IT

"When life knocks you down, try to land on your back.
Because if you can look up, you can get up."
– Les Brown

If you're in the category of struggling to pay the mortgage, the rent, your car bills and thinking about how you will fund your next holiday to keep up with your friends' lifestyle, then think yourself lucky; you're already rich compared to billions of people around the world.

I remember several years ago watching a TV programme on British teenagers who went to Africa to experience working in an unfamiliar environment.

One job that the African children were doing consisted of standing in one spot, in a large pit, for eight hours. The person below them would then hand them a bucket, and then they would hand it to the person standing above them.

It was part of a long human chain.

If my memory serves me, they were at a ruby mine, the bucket was filled with mud at the bottom of this pit, and it was handed from person to person until it reached the top, so other people could look through the mud to see if there were any rubies in it.

And for all of this hard boring work, they got paid around £1 a day. Imagine getting £1 a day for all of that work!

Some people will say yeah, but they can buy things cheaper in those countries, which is true to a point. The food, clothes and cost of living may be cheaper, but if they want to buy a car or jump on a plane for a holiday, it's still as costly for them as it is for us in developed countries.

However, I know it's all well and good saying that you've got lots compared to some guy in Africa working in a mine for £1 a day, but you're going to want more, that's just part of being human.

Let's face it, all of us want more of something.

It could be more years added to our lives, better health, extra money, additional time off work, getting more work, or it could be wanting one of our family members to get better if they're ill.

When I was overweight, unfit, and useless at running, I used to wish that I was naturally fit like a lot of my friends. But, what was once one of my greatest weaknesses has now become one of my biggest strengths.

So, if you come from a tough place physically and mentally, fantastic, the only way is up!

The beauty of going through tough times is that you'll be able to help so many more people get through their tough challenges. If you haven't struggled, then how are you going to relate to other people to help them get through their challenges?

When Arnold Schwarzenegger first tried out for acting, he was criticised because his body was too big, he couldn't speak English very well, he had the wrong accent, and his name was considered uncool and way too long.

Now, all of those things that were considered a hinderance to him, have turned out to be tremendous assets!

If a boy from a small town in Austria that couldn't speak English can become one of the biggest stars in the world, then maybe, just maybe, it's possible for you to make most of your dreams come true too!

Focusing on the positive is easy when everything is going your way, we can all do that, but it's when things aren't going your way that it's far more important to focus on the positive!

Yes, I know most people who know me fairly well think that I'm happy 100% of the time, but the truth is that no one is happy for 100% of the time. Even the Dalai Lama isn't happy all the time, and if you think that that's not true, think about how he feels when he stubs his toe or steps on a plug with his bare feet!

The most important thing is to realise that if you're in a negative state, just know that you can overcome it!

I was listening to Tony Robbins talk one day, and he said that he was taking a seminar when a lady told him all of the things that were going wrong in her life.

She worked herself up, started crying and was in a bad way. Then, Tony interrupted her thought pattern by words to the effect of, "Excuse me, can you stop urinating on yourself!"

She couldn't believe he said that and was taken back by the comment.

He repeated it again, "Can you stop urinating on yourself!"

She stopped feeling sorry for herself and laughed because it was such a bizarre thing to say.

What Tony did was interrupt her negative thought pattern and snapped her out of her negative state! He's done this many times with people.

There was also a situation in which one woman came into his office and started telling him about all of her problems and again, she started crying; Tony (loudly) said, "Excuse me, we haven't started the session yet!"

It snapped her out of her state, and she apologised to him.

What he did was show her that she could come out of that negative state if she interrupted her negative thought pattern, and she could do it in a split second!

You may have a challenging day, and you may not have someone there to snap you out of your state, like Tony did, but the most important thing is to realise that you can put your mind into a better place if you really want to!

We've all seen it where someone goes through a challenging experience like losing a loved one, losing their job or a relationship ending, and they decide to go into self-destruct mode. They hit the pub more, they smoke more, they eat lots of crap, they put on lots of weight and they hold their head down when they're walking down the street. Many people like this feel as if there is no hope left for them and some think, "What's the point of carrying on?"

Some people also want the world to know how bad things are for them. I'm not making light of these life challenges, but the reality is that doing these things will not move you into a better state of mind.

There is a good chance that you have lots of people that care about you and want you to get better, even if you think you have no one that cares. There is always someone that cares, heck I care!

I may have never met you, but as a human being I care about you and want the very best for you!

There are some people who don't like to see others doing well in life and I guess you'll always get that, but I thrive from seeing people achieve great things and create a better life, not only for themselves but for other people around them.

You can change your mental state at any given moment, so when you're feeling low, realise that you can snap out of it at any time you choose to!

"Control your thoughts. Decide about that what you think and concentrate upon. You are in charge of your life to the degree you take charge of your thoughts."
– Earl Nightingale

CHAPTER 13

ASK YOURSELF EMPOWERING QUESTIONS

"To raise new questions, new possibilities, to regard all problems from a new angle, requires creative imagination and marks a real advance."
– Albert Einstein

The questions you ask yourself will have an enormous impact on the quality of your life!

It's believed that we have 60,000 thoughts a day, so the questions you ask yourself will have a phenomenal impact on your own mental health!

We all say negative things to ourselves at certain points throughout our lives or throughout the day, and the more we are aware of this, the more likely we are to change things around for the better.

Just by reading this book you will become more aware of how important it is to ask yourself the right questions. I'm not the first person to come up with this concept, and I won't be the last either, as it's fundamental to living a happy and healthy life!

People who have mastered their mind to a certain extent are aware of this, and even though this isn't the world's biggest secret, it is still unknown to many people!

I was listening to a podcast that had the bestselling author Russell Blake on it.

Russell said,

"The questions that you ask yourself tend to get different answers. So, if the question you're asking yourself is, "How can I write six novels this year and have a blast doing it?" You're going to get a completely different answer than asking, "How in the name of God am I ever going to write six novels?"

Russell is aware of the power his questions have, so he structures them to get a better outcome for himself.

Here is a list of some empowering questions that you can ask yourself to help you become mentally stronger and live a better life:

- Why is today a great day?

- Why is my life so good compared to billions of other people around the world?

- Why am I so confident compared to less confident people?

- Why am I so awesome?

- Why am I so healthy compared to others less fortunate?

- Why am I so loved?

- What can I learn from my last challenging situation?

- How can I gain power from experiences?

- What can I be thankful for in my life?

- What have I done today that will improve my life?

- What am I proud of that I have accomplished?

- What did I accomplish that makes me feel good?

- What motivates me?

- What lifts my spirits?

- How can you be kinder to other people?

- Why have I got so much compared to how little some others have?

- What can I look forward to?

- Why are there so many possibilities for me?

- Why am I lucky enough to live in this country?

- What makes me feel more attractive?

- What am I good at?

- How can I be kind to myself?

- What can I do to make myself healthier?

- What can I do to make myself fitter?

- What do I need to focus on to improve my life?

- What am I brilliant at?

- What things can I improve about my life?

- What work could I do that I know I would love?

- What have people that have succeeded in the area that I want to succeed in, done to get there?

- What are the steps that I can take today to making

my dream work possible?

- Who can I help today?

- What inspirational post can I put on social media?

- How many things can I appreciate today?

- Why am I so lucky to have some friends when others have none?

- How much can I love who I am today?

- What's good about the weather I'm experiencing now?

- What would I do with my life if I wasn't afraid of anything?

- How can I inspire other people?

- What does success look like to me?

- What movies make me feel good?

- What books make me feel good?

- What countries have I been to that I enjoyed?

- What music makes me feel good?

- What animals do I love?

- What sport makes me feel good?

- What type of exercise makes me feel good?

- What friends do I have that make me feel good?

- What family do I have that care about me?

- What countries can I go to that I know I would love?

- What form of transport do I enjoy the most?

- Why am I so lucky?

- What would I do if I had more money?

- How can I get inspired?

- How can I remain positive?

- What does the most successful version of me look like?

- What does the most loved version of me look like?

- How can I take steps to make this possible?

- Why am I a lot luckier than so many people in this world?

So ask yourself empowering questions and create a better reality for yourself!

"What lies behind you and what lies in front of you, pales in comparison to what lies inside you."
– Ralph Waldo Emerson

ACKNOWLEDGEMENTS

It's almost impossible to say how many people have helped me along the way with producing this book, and if you're not in the acknowledgements just know that I am very grateful for your support and help.

However, I would like to say a massive THANK YOU to a few people that I can think of, off the top of my head:

Paul 'The Viking' Hughes, Tom Webb, Eva Savage, Mark 'Billy' Billingham, Julie Colombino-Billingham, Tracy, Kay and Maria Morris, Cheryl Hicks, Jamie Baulch, Gene Hipgrave, Tom Hughes, Kauri-Romet Aadamsoo, Mark Dawson, Craig Martelle, Michael Anderle, Michael and Emma Byrne, Paul 'Faz' Farrington, Paul Heaney, James Atkinson and Laura Taylor.

Also, a huge THANKS to 'The Mark Llewhellin Advance Reader Team' for taking the time to read the manuscript and make suggestions.

Live Your Dreams!

Mark

ABOUT THE AUTHOR

In 1990, Mark Llewhellin left school without knowing his grades. He had little confidence and was not at all optimistic about his future.

Not knowing what to do with his life Mark followed some of his friends into the Army. He failed his basic 1.5-mile run, was bullied, and was also voted the fattest person in the Troop!

After a year with the Junior Leaders Regiment Royal Artillery, Mark decided he would try and get into 29 Commando Regiment Royal Artillery, which is an elite Army Commando Regiment that at the time proudly held the Military Marathon World Record (i.e. a marathon carrying a 40lbs backpack).

After failing the 29 Commando Selection phase (called 'The Beat Up') twice, first through lack of fitness and secondly through an injury, Mark subsequently passed on his third attempt and completed the 'All Arms Commando Course' on his first attempt.

Mark later went on to achieve the following:

- Break the 100-kilometre Treadmill World Record.

- Place 1st in the Strava Distance Challenge in 2015 competing against over 51,000 runners.

- Place 1st in the Strava Distance Challenge in 2014 competing against over 40,000 runners.

- Run and walk 70-miles without training on his 40th birthday.

- Become a successful Personal Fitness Trainer.

- Complete the Marathon Des Sables (a six-day, 135-mile ultra-marathon in the Sahara Desert).

- Work and live in London's exclusive Park Lane as a Bodyguard.

- Run 1,620 miles in the United States whilst carrying a 35lbs pack.

Mark has interviewed some of the world's top performers and high achievers in various locations, including one of the world's most prestigious memorabilia rooms…the Hard Rock Café Vault Room in London.

He has travelled to over 50 countries and has been featured in leading national newspapers and on TV for his running achievements.

Mark has extensively worked in the support and care industry for many years helping individuals with brain injury, autism, epilepsy, dyspraxia, and various types of learning difficulties.

He is the Managing Director of Mark 7 Productions, as well as the Producer and Host of 'An Audience with Mark Billy Billingham' speaking events around the UK.

Mark is currently working on more personal development books and lives with his son Léon (when Léon's not at his Mum's) on a beautiful marina in South West Wales.

ALSO BY MARK LLEWHELLIN

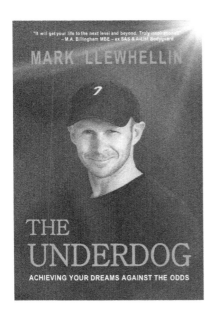

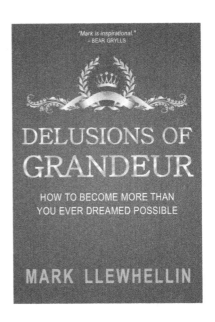

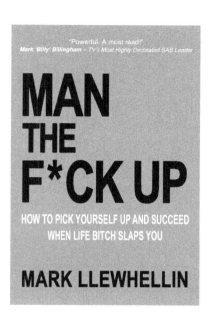

MAN THE F*CK UP

HOW TO PICK YOURSELF UP AND SUCCEED
WHEN LIFE BITCH SLAPS YOU

MARK LLEWHELLIN

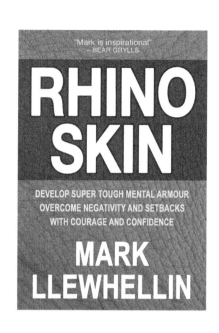

RHINO SKIN

DEVELOP SUPER TOUGH MENTAL ARMOUR
OVERCOME NEGATIVITY AND SETBACKS
WITH COURAGE AND CONFIDENCE

MARK LLEWHELLIN

NUMBER 1 BESTSELLING AUTHOR

STAY STRONG

ELIMINATE NEGATIVE THINKING AND BECOME
A STRONGER AND MORE POSITIVE PERSON

MARK LLEWHELLIN

PUT YOUR BIG BOY PANTS ON

HOW TO MASTER YOUR MIND AND EMOTIONS
BUILD SUPERIOR MENTAL TOUGHNESS
THINK POSITIVE AND LIVE THE GOOD LIFE

MARK LLEWHELLIN

**SMALL CHANGES
REMARKABLE RESULTS**

TIME TO
TOUGHEN
UP

**DEVELOP IMMENSE INNER STRENGTH AND CONFIDENCE
OVERCOME CHALLENGES AND ACHIEVE YOUR GOALS**

MARK
LLEWHELLIN

JUST

MARK LLEWHELLIN

KEEP

**THE POWER OF POSITIVE THINKING
PATIENCE AND PERSISTENCE**

GOING

**AN EASY GUIDE TO ACHIEVING YOUR GOALS
AND TRANSFORMING YOUR LIFE**

JUST GO
FOR IT

MARK
LLEWHELLIN

NO
F*CKS
GIVEN

**BEING YOURSELF IN A WORLD WHERE
PEOPLE WANT YOU TO BE SOMEONE ELSE**

MARK LLEWHELLIN

GET TWO FREE MARK LLEWHELLIN BOOKS AND DEALS AND UPDATES

Join 'The Mark Llewhellin Advance Reader Team' for information on new books and deals plus:

You can pick up FREE copies of Mark's five star reviewed books:

1. 'The Underdog'

2. 'Delusions of Grandeur'

Simply go to Mark's website at www.markllewhellin.com and sign up for FREE.

DISCLAIMER

Although the author and publisher have made every effort to ensure that the information contained in this book was accurate at the time of release, the author and publisher do not assume and hereby disclaim any liability to any party for any loss, damage, or disruption caused by errors or omissions in this book, whether such errors or omissions result from negligence, accident, or any other cause.

IF YOU ENJOYED THIS BOOK

Your help in spreading the word about Mark's books is greatly appreciated and your reviews make a huge difference to help new readers change their lives for the better.

If you found this book useful please leave a review on the platform you purchased it on.

Printed in Great Britain
by Amazon

17098432R00098